FARM BALLADS.

"DRAW UP THE PAPERS, LAWYER, AND MAKE 'EM GOOD AND STOUT."

[Page 17

FARM BALLADS.

By WILL CARLETON.

ILLUSTRATED.

APPLEWOOD BOOKS
BEDFORD, MASSACHUSETTS

TO

MY MOTHER.

Thank you for purchasing an Applewood Book.
Applewood reprints America's lively classics—
books from the past that are still of interest
to modern readers. For a free copy of our
current catalog, write to:
Applewood Books
P.O. Box 365
Bedford, MA 01730

ISBN 1-55709-579-5

Library of Congress Control Number: 2001097625

PREFACE.

THESE poems have been written under various, and, in some cases, difficult, conditions; in the open air, "with team afield;" in the student's den, with the ghosts of unfinished lessons hovering gloomily about; amid the rush and roar of railroad travel, which trains of thought are not prone to follow; and in the editor's sanctum, where the dainty feet of the Muses do not often deign to tread.

Crude and unfinished as they are, the author has yet had the assurance to publish them, from time to time, in different periodicals, in which, it is but just to admit, they have been met by the people with unexpected favor. While his judgment has often failed to endorse the kind words spoken for them, he has naturally not felt it in his heart to file any remonstrances.

He has been asked, by friends in all parts of the country, to put his poems into a more durable form than they have hitherto possessed; and it is in accordance with these requests that he now presents " Farm Ballads " to the public.

Of course he does not expect to escape, what he needs so greatly, the discipline of severe criticism ; for he is aware that he has often wandered out of the beaten track, and has many times been too regardless of the established rules of rhythm, in his (oftentimes vain) search for the flowers of poesy.

But he believes that The People are, after all, the true critics, and will soon ascertain whether there are more good than poor things in a book; and whatever may be their verdict in this case, he has made up his mind to be happy.

W. C.

CONTENTS.

—◇◇—

FARM BALLADS.

—◇◇—

OTHER POEMS.

ILLUSTRATIONS.

—◇◇◇—

FARM BALLADS.

FARM BALLADS.

BETSEY AND I ARE OUT.

DRAW up the papers, lawyer, and make 'em good and stout;
For things at home are crossways, and Betsey and I are out.
We, who have worked together so long as man and wife,
Must pull in single harness for the rest of our nat'ral life.

"What is the matter?" say you. I swan it's hard to tell!
Most of the years behind us we've passed by very well;
I have no other woman, she has no other man—
Only we've lived together as long as we ever can.

So I have talked with Betsey, and Betsey has talked with me,
And so we've agreed together that we can't never agree;
Not that we've catched each other in any terrible crime;
We've been a-gathering this for years, a little at a time.

There was a stock of temper we both had for a start,
Although we never suspected 'twould take us two apart;
I had my various failings, bred in the flesh and bone;
And Betsey, like all good women, had a temper of her own.

The first thing I remember whereon we disagreed
Was something concerning heaven—a difference in our creed;
We arg'ed the thing at breakfast, we arg'ed the thing at tea,
And the more we arg'ed the question the more we didn't agree.

And the next that I remember was when we lost a cow;
She had kicked the bucket for certain, the question was only—How?
I held my own opinion, and Betsey another had;
And when we were done a-talkin', we both of us was mad.

And the next that I remember, it started in a joke;
But full for a week it lasted, and neither of us spoke.
And the next was when I scolded because she broke a bowl,
And she said I was mean and stingy, and hadn't any soul.

And so that bowl kept pourin' dissensions in our cup;
And so that blamed cow-critter was always a-comin' up;
And so that heaven we arg'ed no nearer to us got,
But it gave us a taste of somethin' a thousand times as hot.

And so the thing kept workin', and all the self-same way;
Always somethin' to arg'e, and somethin' sharp to say;
And down on us came the neighbors, a couple dozen strong,
And lent their kindest sarvice for to help the thing along.

And there has been days together—and many a weary week—
We was both of us cross and spunky, and both too proud to speak;
And I have been thinkin' and thinkin', the whole of the winter and fall,
If I can't live kind with a woman, why, then, I won't at all.

And so I have talked with Betsey, and Betsey has talked with me,
And we have agreed together that we can't never agree;
And what is hers shall be hers, and what is mine shall be mine;
And I'll put it in the agreement, and take it to her to sign.

Write on the paper, lawyer—the very first paragraph—
Of all the farm and live-stock that she shall have her half;
For she has helped to earn it, through many a weary day,
And it's nothing more than justice that Betsey has her pay.

Give her the house and homestead—a man can thrive and roam;
But women are skeery critters, unless they have a home;
And I have always determined, and never failed to say,
That Betsey never should want a home if I was taken away.

There is a little hard money that's drawin' tol'rable pay:
A couple of hundred dollars laid by for a rainy day;
Safe in the hands of good men, and easy to get at;
Put in another clause there, and give her half of that.

Yes, I see you smile, Sir, at my givin' her so much;
Yes, divorce is cheap, Sir, but I take no stock in such!
True and fair I married her, when she was blithe and young;
And Betsey was al'ays good to me, exceptin' with her tongue.

Once, when I was young as you, and not so smart, perhaps,
For me she mittened a lawyer, and several other chaps;
And all of them was flustered, and fairly taken down,
And I for a time was counted the luckiest man in town.

Once when I had a fever—I won't forget it soon—
I was hot as a basted turkey and crazy as a loon;
Never an hour went by me when she was out of sight—
She nursed me true and tender, and stuck to me day and night.

And if ever a house was tidy, and ever a kitchen clean,
Her house and kitchen was tidy as any I ever seen;
And I don't complain of Betsey, or any of her acts,
Exceptin' when we've quarreled, and told each other facts.

So draw up the paper, lawyer, and I'll go home to-night,
And read the agreement to her, and see if it's all right;
And then, in the mornin', I'll sell to a tradin' man I know,
And kiss the child that was left to us, and out in the world I'll go.

And one thing put in the paper, that first to me didn't occur:
That when I am dead at last she'll bring me back to her;
And lay me under the maples I planted years ago,
When she and I was happy before we quarreled so.

And when she dies I wish that she would be laid by me,
And, lyin' together in silence, perhaps we will agree;
And, if ever we meet in heaven, I wouldn't think it queer
If we loved each other the better because we quarreled here.

HOW BETSEY AND I MADE UP.

GIVE us your hand, Mr. Lawyer: how do you do to-day?
You drew up that paper—I s'pose you want your pay.
Don't cut down your figures; make it an X or a V;
For that 'ere written agreement was just the makin' of me.

"GIVE US YOUR HAND, MR. LAWYER: HOW DO YOU DO TO-DAY?"

Goin' home that evenin' I tell you I was blue,
Thinkin' of all my troubles, and what I was goin' to do;
And if my hosses hadn't been the steadiest team alive,
They'd 've tipped me over, certain, for I couldn't see where to drive.

No—for I was laborin' under a heavy load;
No—for I was travelin' an entirely different road;
For I was a-tracin' over the path of our lives ag'in,
And seein' where we missed the way, and where we might have been.

And many a corner we'd turned that just to a quarrel led,
When I ought to 've held my temper, and driven straight ahead;
And the more I thought it over the more these memories came,
And the more I struck the opinion that I was the most to blame.

And things I had long forgotten kept risin' in my mind,
Of little matters betwixt us, where Betsey was good and kind;
And these things flashed all through me, as you know things sometimes will
When a feller's alone in the darkness, and every thing is still.

"But," says I, "we're too far along to take another track,
And when I put my hand to the plow I do not oft turn back;

"AND JUST AS I TURNED A HILL-TOP I SEE THE KITCHEN LIGHT."

And 'tain't an uncommon thing now for couples to smash in two;"
And so I set my teeth together, and vowed I'd see it through.

When I come in sight o' the house 'twas some'at in the night,
And just as I turned a hill-top I see the kitchen light;
Which often a han'some pictur' to a hungry person makes,
But it don't interest a feller much that's goin' to pull up stakes.

"AND INTENTLY READIN' A NEWSPAPER, A-HOLDIN' IT WRONG SIDE UP."

And when I went in the house the table was set for me—
As good a supper's I ever saw, or ever want to see;
And I crammed the agreement down my pocket as well as I could,
And fell to eatin' my victuals, which somehow didn't taste good.

And Betsey, she pretended to look about the house,
But she watched my side coat pocket like a cat would watch a mouse;
And then she went to foolin' a little with her cup,
And intently readin' a newspaper, a-holdin' it wrong side up.

"AND KISSED ME FOR THE FIRST TIME IN OVER TWENTY YEARS!"

And when I'd done my supper I drawed the agreement out,
And give it to her without a word, for she knowed what 'twas about;
And then I hummed a little tune, but now and then a note
Was bu'sted by some animal that hopped up in my throat.

Then Betsey she got her specs from off the mantel-shelf,
And read the article over quite softly to herself;
Read it by little and little, for her eyes is gettin' old,
And lawyers' writin' ain't no print, especially when it's cold.

And after she'd read a little she give my arm a touch,
And kindly said she was afraid I was 'lowin' her too much;
But when she was through she went for me, her face a-streamin' with tears,
And kissed me for the first time in over twenty years!

l don't know what you'll think, Sir—I didn't come to inquire—
But I picked up that agreement and stuffed it in the fire;

And I told her we'd bury the hatchet alongside of the cow;
And we struck an agreement never to have another row.

And I told her in the future I wouldn't speak cross or rash
If half the crockery in the house was broken all to smash;
And she said, in regards to heaven, we'd try and learn its worth
By startin' a branch establishment and runnin' it here on earth.

And so we sat a-talkin' three-quarters of the night,
And opened our hearts to each other until they both grew light;
And the days when I was winnin' her away from so many men
Was nothin' to that evenin' I courted her over again.

Next mornin' an ancient virgin took pains to call on us,
Her lamp all trimmed and a-burnin' to kindle another fuss;
But when she went to pryin' and openin' of old sores,
My Betsey rose politely, and showed her out-of-doors.

"MY BETSEY ROSE POLITELY, AND SHOWED HER OUT-OF-DOORS."

Since then I don't deny but there's been a word or two;
But we've got our eyes wide open, and know just what to do:
When one speaks cross the other just meets it with a laugh,
And the first one's ready to give up considerable more than half.

Maybe you'll think me soft, Sir, a-talkin' in this style,
But somehow it does me lots of good to tell it once in a while;

And I do it for a compliment—'tis so that you can see
That that there written agreement of yours was just the makin' of me.

So make out your bill, Mr. Lawyer: don't stop short of an X;
Make it more if you want to, for I have got the checks.
I'm richer than a National Bank, with all its treasures told,
For I've got a wife at home now that's worth her weight in gold.

GONE WITH A HANDSOMER MAN.

JOHN.

I've worked in the field all day, a-plowin' the "stony streak;"
I've scolded my team till I'm hoarse; I've tramped till my legs are weak·
I've choked a dozen swears (so's not to tell Jane fibs)
When the piow-p'int struck a stone and the handles punched my ribs.

I've put my team in the barn, and rubbed their sweaty coats;
I've fed 'em a heap of hay and half a bushel of oats;
And to see the way they ont makes me like eatin' feel,
And Jane won't say to-night that I don't make out a meal.

Well said! the door is locked! but here she's left the key,
Under the step, in a place known only to her and me;
I wonder who's dyin' or dead, that she's hustled off pell-mell:
But here on the table's a note, and probably this will tell.

Good God! my wife is gone! my wife is gone astray!
The letter it says, "Good-bye, for I'm a-going away;
I've lived with you six months, John, and so far I've been true;
But I'm going away to-day with a handsomer man than you."

A han'somer man than me! Why, that ain't much to say;
There's han'somer men than me go past here every day.
There's han'somer men than me—I ain't of the han'some kind;
But a *lovin'er* man than I was I guess she'll never find.

Curse her! curse her! I say, and give my curses wings!
May tne words of love I've spoke be changed to scorpion stings!
Oh, she filled my heart with joy, she emptied my heart of doubt,
And now, with a scratch of a pen, she lets my heart's blood out!

Curse her! curse her! say I; she'll some time rue this day;
She'll some time learn that hate is a game that two can play;
And long before she dies she'll grieve she ever was born;
And I'll plow her grave with hate, and seed it down to scorn!

As sure as the world goes on, there'll come a time when she
Will read the devilish heart of that han'somer man than me;
And there'll be a time when he will find, as others do,
That she who is false to one can be the same with two.

And when her face grows pale, and when her eyes grow dim,
And when he is tired of her and she is tired of him,
She'll do what she ought to have done, and coolly count the cost;
And then she'll see things clear, and know what she has lost.

And thoughts that are now asleep will wake up in her mind,
And she will mourn and cry for what she has left behind;
And maybe she'll sometimes long for me—for me—but no!
I've blotted her out of my heart, and I will not have it so.

And yet in her girlish heart there was somethin' or other she had
That fastened a man to her, and wasn't entirely bad;
And she loved me a little, I think, although it didn't last;
But I mustn't think of these things—I've buried 'em in the past.

I'll take my hard words back, nor make a bad matter worse;
She'll have trouble enough; she shall not have my curse;
But I'll live a life so square—and I well know that I can—
That she always will sorry be that she went with that han'somer man

Ah, here is her kitchen dress! it makes my poor eyes blur;
It seems, when I look at that, as if 'twas holdin' her.
And here are her week-day shoes, and there is her week-day hat,
And yonder's her weddin' gown: I wonder she didn't take that.

'Twas only this mornin' she came and called me her "dearest dear,"
And said I was makin' for her a regular paradise here;
O God! if you want a man to sense the pains of hell,
Before you pitch him in just keep him in heaven a spell!

"CURSE HER! CURSE HER! SAY ; SHE'LL SOME TIME RUE THIS DAY!"

Good-bye! I wish that death had severed us two apart.
You've lost a worshiper here—you've crushed a lovin' heart.
I'll worship no woman again; but I guess I'll learn to pray,
And kneel as *you* used to kneel before you run away.

And if I thought I could bring my words on heaven to bear,
And if I thought I had some little influence there,
I would pray that I might be, if it only could be so,
As happy and gay as I was a half an hour ago.

JANE (*entering*).

Why, John, what a litter here! you've thrown things all around!
Come, what's the matter now? and what 've you lost or found?
And here's my father here, a-waiting for supper, too;
I've been a-riding with him—he's that "handsomer man than you."

Ha! ha! Pa, take a seat, while I put the kettle on,
And get things ready for tea, and kiss my dear old John.
Why, John, you look so strange! Come, what has crossed your track?
I was only a-joking, you know; I'm willing to take it back.

JOHN (*aside*).

Well, now, if this *ain't* a joke, with rather a bitter cream!
It seems as if I'd woke from a mighty ticklish dream;
And I think she "smells a rat," for she smiles at me so queer;
I hope she don't; good Lord! I hope that they didn't hear!

'Twas one of her practical drives—she thought I'd understand!
But I'll never break sod again till I get the lay of the land.
But one thing's settled with me—to appreciate heaven well,
'Tis good for a man to have some fifteen minutes of hell.

"WHY, JOHN, WHAT A LITTER HERE! YOU'VE THROWN THINGS ALL AROUND!"

3

JOHNNY RICH.

RAISE the light a little, Jim,
For it's getting rather dim,
And, with such a storm a-howlin', 'twill not do to douse the glim.
Hustle down the curtains, Lu;
Poke the fire a little, Su;
This is somethin' of a flurry, mother, somethin' of a—whew!

Goodness gracious, how it pours!
How it beats ag'in the doors!
You will have a hard one, Jimmy, when you go to do the chores!
Do not overfeed the gray;
Give a plenty to the bay;
And be careful with your lantern when you go among the hay.

See the horses have a bed
When you've got 'em fairly fed;
Feed the cows that's in the stable, and the sheep that's in the shed;
Give the spotted cow some meal,
Where the brindle can not steal;
For she's greedy as a porker, and as slipp'ry as an eel.

Hang your lantern by the ring,
On a nail, or on a string;
For the Durham calf 'll bunt it, if there's any such a thing:
He's a handsome one to see,
And a knowin' one is he:
I stooped over t'other morning, and he up and went for me!

Rover thinks he hears a noise!
Just keep still a minute, boys;
Nellie, hold your tongue a second, and be silent with your toys.

Stop that barkin', now, you whelp,
 Or I'll kick you till you yelp!
Yes, I hear it; 'tis somebody that's callin' out for help.

 Get the lantern, Jim and Tom;
 Mother, keep the babies calm,
And we'll follow up that halloa, and we'll see where it is from.
 'Tis a hairy sort of night
 For a man to face and fight;
And the wind is blowin'— Hang it, Jimmy, bring another light.

 * * * * * * * * * *

 Ah! 'twas you, then, Johnny Rich,
 Yelling out at such a pitch,
For a decent man to help you, while you fell into the ditch:
 'Tisn't quite the thing to say,
 But we ought to've let you lay,
While your drunken carcass died a-drinkin' water any way.

 And to see you on my floor,
 And to hear the way you snore,
Now we've lugged you under shelter, and the danger all is o'er;
 And you lie there, quite resigned,
 Whisky deaf, and whisky blind,
And it will not hurt your feelin's, so I guess I'll free my mind.

 Do you mind, you thievin' dunce,
 How you robbed my orchard once,
Takin' all the biggest apples, leavin' all the littlest runts?
 Do you mind my melon-patch—
 How you gobbled the whole batch,
Stacked the vines, and sliced the greenest melons, just to raise the scratch?

 Do you think, you drunken wag,
 It was any thing to brag,
To be cornered in my hen-roost, with two pullets in a bag?
 You are used to dirty dens;
 You have often slept in pens;
I've a mind to take you out there now, and roost you with the hens!

"'TIS A HAIRY SORT OF NIGHT FOR A MAN TO FACE AND FIGHT."

Do you call to mind with me
How, one night, you and your three
Took my wagon all to pieces for to hang it on a tree?
How you hung it up, you eels,
Straight and steady, by the wheels?
I've a mind to take you out there now, and hang you by your heels!

How, the Fourth of last July,
When you got a little high,
You went back of Wilson's counter when you thought he wasn't nigh?
How he heard some specie chink,
And was on you in a wink,
And you promised if he'd hush it that you never more would drink?

"WHEN YOU WALKED WITH HER ON SUNDAY, LOOKING SOBER, STRAIGHT, AND CLEAN."

Do you mind our temperance hall?
How you're always sure to call,
And recount your reformation with the biggest speech of all?
How you talk, and how you sing,
That the pledge is just the thing—
How you sign it every winter, and then smash it every spring?

Do you mind how Jennie Green
Was as happy as a queen
When you walked with her on Sunday, looking sober, straight, and clean?
How she cried out half her sight,
When you staggered by, next night,
Twice as dirty as a serpent, and a hundred times as tight?

How our hearts with pleasure warmed
When your mother, though it stormed.
Run up here one day to tell us that you truly had reformed?
How that very self-same day,
When upon her homeward way,
She run on you, where you'd hidden, full three-quarters o'er the bay?

Oh, you little whisky-keg!
Oh, you horrid little egg!
You're goin' to destruction with your swiftest foot and leg!
I've a mind to take you out
Underneath the water-spout,
Just to rinse you up a little, so you'll know what you're about!

But you've got a handsome eye,
And, although I can't tell why,
Somethin' somewhere in you always lets you get another try:
So, for all that I have said,
I'll not douse you; but, instead,
I will strip you, I will rub you, I will put you into bed!

"AND YOU LIE THERE, QUITE RESIGNED, WHISKY DEAF, AND WHISKY BLIND."

OUT OF THE OLD HOUSE, NANCY.

OUT of the old house, Nancy—moved up into the new;
All the hurry and worry is just as good as through.
Only a bounden duty remains for you and I—
And that's to stand on the door-step, here, and bid the old house good bye.

"AND BID THE OLD HOUSE GOOD-BYE."

What a shell we've lived in, these nineteen or twenty years!
Wonder it hadn't smashed in, and tumbled about our ears;
Wonder it's stuck together, and answered till to-day;
But every individual log was put up here to stay.

Things looked rather new, though, when this old house was built;
And things that blossomed you would 've made some women wilt;
And every other day, then, as sure as day would break,
My neighbor Ager come this way, invitin' me to "shake."

And you, for want of neighbors, was sometimes blue and sad,
For wolves and bears and wild-cats was the nearest ones you had;
But lookin' ahead to the clearin', we worked with all our might,
Until we was fairly out of the woods, and things was goin' right.

Look up there at our new house!—ain't it a thing to see?
Tall and big and handsome, and new as new can be;
All in apple-pie order, especially the shelves,
And never a debt to say but what we own it all ourselves.

Look at our old log-house—how little it now appears!
But it's never gone back on us for nineteen or twenty years;
An' I won't go back on it now, or go to pokin' fun—
There's such a thing as praisin' a thing for the good that it has done.

Probably you remember how rich we was that night,
When we was fairly settled, an' had things snug and tight:
We feel as proud as you please, Nancy, over our house that's new,
But we felt as proud under this old roof, and a good deal prouder, too.

Never a handsomer house was seen beneath the sun:
Kitchen and parlor and bedroom—we had 'em all in one;
And the fat old wooden clock that we bought when we come West,
Was tickin' away in the corner there, and doin' its level best.

Trees was all around us, a-whisperin' cheering words;
Loud was the squirrel's chatter, and sweet the songs of birds;
And home grew sweeter and brighter—our courage began to mount—
And things looked hearty and happy then, and work appeared to count.

And here one night it happened, when things was goin' bad,
We fell in a deep old quarrel—the first we ever had;
And when you give out and cried, then I, like a fool, give in,
And then we agreed to rub all out, and start the thing ag'in.

"SETTLERS COME TO SEE THAT SHOW A HALF A DOZEN MILES."

Here it was, you remember, we sat when the day was done,
And you was a-makin' clothing *that wasn't for either one;*
And often a soft word of love I was soft enough to say,
And the wolves was howlin' in the woods not twenty rods away.

Then our first-born baby—a regular little joy,
Though I fretted a little because it wasn't a boy:
Wa'n't she a little flirt, though, with all her pouts and smiles?
Why, settlers come to see that show a half a dozen miles.

Yonder sat the cradle—a homely, home-made thing,
And many a night I rocked it, providin' you would sing;
And many a little squatter brought up with us to stay—
And so that cradle, for many a year, was never put away.

How they kept a-comin', so cunnin' and fat and small!
How they growed! 'twas a wonder how we found room for 'em all;
But though the house was crowded, it empty seemed that day
When Jennie lay by the fire-place, there, and moaned her life away.

And right in there the preacher, with Bible and hymn-book, stood,
"'Twixt the dead and the living," and "hoped 'twould do us good:'
And the little whitewood coffin on the table there was set,
And now as I rub my eyes it seems as if I could see it yet.

Then that fit of sickness it brought on you, you know;
Just by a thread you hung, and you e'en-a'most let go;
And here is the spot I tumbled, an' give the Lord his due,
When the doctor said the fever'd turned, an' he could fetch you through.

Yes, a deal has happened to make this old house dear:
Christenin's, funerals, weddin's—what haven't we had here?
Not a log in this buildin' but its memories has got,
And not a nail in this old floor but touches a tender spot.

Out of the old house, Nancy—moved up into the new;
All the hurry and worry is just as good as through;
But I tell you a thing right here, that I ain't ashamed to say,
There's precious things in this old house we never can take away.

Here the old house will stand, but not as it stood before:
Winds will whistle through it, and rains will flood the floor;
And over the hearth, once blazing, the snow-drifts oft will pile,
And the old thing will seem to be a-mournin' all the while.

Fare you well, old house! you're naught that can feel or see.
But you seem like a human being—a dear old friend to me;
And we never will have a better home, if *my* opinion stands,
Until we commence a-keepin' house in the house not made with hands.

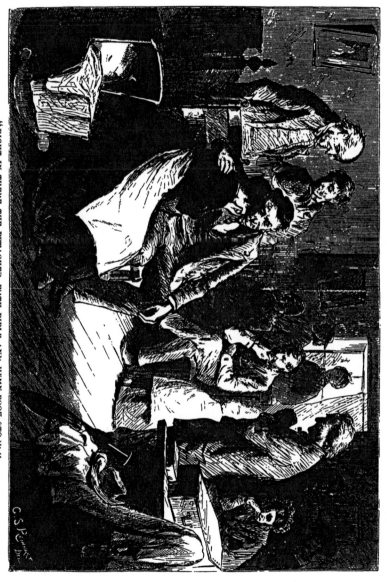

"RIGHT IN THERE THE PREACHER, WITH BIBLE AND HYMN-BOOK STOOD."

4

OVER THE HILL TO THE POOR-HOUSE.

OVER the hill to the poor-house I'm trudgin' my weary way—
I, a woman of seventy, and only a trifle gray—
I, who am smart an' chipper, for all the years I've told,
As many another woman that's only half as old.

"OVER THE HILL TO THE POOR-HOUSE, I'M TRUDGIN' MY WEARY WAY."

Over the hill to the poor-house—I can't quite make it clear!
Over the hill to the poor-house—it seems so horrid queer!
Many a step I've taken a-toilin' to and fro,
But this is a sort of journey I never thought to go.

What is the use of heapin' on me a pauper's shame?
Am I lazy or crazy? am I blind or lame?
True, I am not so supple, nor yet so awful stout;
But charity ain't no favor, if one can live without.

I am willin' and anxious an' ready any day
To work for a decent livin', an' pay my honest way;
For I can earn my victuals, an' more too, I'll be bound,
If any body only is willin' to have me round.

Once I was young an' han'some—I was, upon my soul—
Once my cheeks was roses, my eyes as black as coal;
And I can't remember, in them days, of hearin' people say,
For any kind of a reason, that I was in their way.

'Tain't no use of boastin', or talkin' over free,
But many a house an' home was open then to me;
Many a han'some offer I had from likely men,
And nobody ever hinted that I was a burden then.

And when to John I was married, sure he was good and smart,
But he and all the neighbors would own I done my part;
For life was all before me, an' I was young an' strong,
And I worked the best that I could in tryin' to get along.

And so we worked together: and life was hard, but gay,
With now and then a baby for to cheer us on our way;
Till we had half a dozen, an' all growed clean an' neat,
An' went to school like others, an' had enough to eat.

So we worked for the child'rn, and raised 'em every one;
Worked for 'em summer and winter, just as we ought to 've done;
Only perhaps we humored 'em, which some good folks condemn,
But every couple's child'rn's a heap the best to them.

"TILL AT LAST HE WENT A-COURTIN', AND BROUGHT A WIFE FROM TOWN."

Strange how much we think of our blessed little ones!—
I'd have died for my daughters, I'd have died for my sons;
And God he made that rule of love; but when we're old and gray,
I've noticed it sometimes somehow fails to work the other way.

Strange, another thing: when our boys an' girls was grown,
And when, exceptin' Charley, they'd left us there alone;
When John he nearer an' nearer come, an' dearer seemed to be,
The Lord of Hosts he come one day an' took him away from me.

Still I was bound to struggle, an' never to cringe or fall—
Still I worked for Charley, for Charley was now my all;
And Charley was pretty good to me, with scarce a word or frown,
Till at last he went a-courtin', and brought a wife from town.

She was somewhat dressy, an' hadn't a pleasant smile—
She was quite conceity, and carried a heap o' style;
But if ever I tried to be friends, I did with her, I know;
But she was hard and proud, an' I couldn't make it go.

She had an edication, an' that was good for her;
But when she twitted me on mine, 'twas carryin' things too fur;
An' I told her once, 'fore company (an' it almost made her sick),
That I never swallowed a grammar, or 'et a 'rithmetic.

So 'twas only a few days before the thing was done—
They was a family of themselves, and I another one;
And a very little cottage one family will do,
But I never have seen a house that was big enough for two.

An' I never could speak to suit her, never could please her eye,
An' it made me independent, an' then I didn't try;
But I was terribly staggered, an' felt it like a blow,
When Charley turned ag'in me, an' told me I could go.

I went to live with Susan, but Susan's house was small,
And she was always a-hintin' how snug it was for us all;
And what with her husband's sisters, and what with child'rn three,
'Twas easy to discover that there wasn't room for me.

An' then I went to Thomas, the oldest son I've got,
For Thomas's buildings 'd cover the half of an acre lot;
But all the child'rn was on me—I couldn't stand their sauce—
And Thomas said I needn't think I was comin' there to boss.

An' then I wrote to Rebecca, my girl who lives out West,
And to Isaac, not far from her—some twenty miles at best;
And one of 'em said 'twas too warm there for any one so old,
And t'other had an opinion the climate was too cold.

So they have shirked and slighted me, an' shifted me about—
So they have well-nigh soured me, an' wore my old heart out;
But still I've borne up pretty well, an' wasn't much put down,
Till Charley went to the poor-master, an' put me on the town.

Over the hill to the poor-house—my child'rn dear, good-by!
Many a night I've watched you when only God was nigh;
And God 'll judge between us; but I will al'ays pray
That you shall never suffer the half I do to-day.

"MANY A NIGHT I'VE WATCHED YOU WHEN ONLY GOD WAS NIGH."

OVER THE HILL FROM THE POOR-HOUSE.

I, WHO was always counted, they say,
Rather a bad stick any way,
Splintered all over with dodges and tricks,
Known as "the worst of the Deacon's six;"
I, the truant, saucy and bold,
The one black sheep in my father's fold,
"Once on a time," as the stories say,
Went over the hill on a winter's day—
    Over the hill to the poor-house.

Tom could save what twenty could earn;
But *givin'* was somethin' he ne'er would learn;
Isaac could half o' the Scriptur's speak—
Committed a hundred verses a week;
Never forgot, an' never slipped;
But "Honor thy father and mother" he skipped;
    So *over the hill to the poor-house.*

As for Susan, her heart was kind
An' good—what there was of it, mind;
Nothin' too big, an' nothin' too nice,
Nothin' she wouldn't sacrifice
For one she loved; an' that 'ere one
Was herself, when all was said an' done.
An' Charley an' 'Becca meant well, no doubt,
But any one could pull 'em about;

An' all o' our folks ranked well, you see,
Save one poor fellow, and that was me;

An' when, one dark an' rainy night,
A neighbor's horse went out o' sight,
They hitched on me, as the guilty chap
That carried one end o' the halter-strap.
An' I think, myself, that view of the case
Wasn't altogether out o' place;
My mother denied it, as mothers do,
But I am inclined to believe 'twas true.
Though for me one thing might be said—
That I, as well as the horse, was led;
And the worst of whisky spurred me on,
Or else the deed would have never been done.
But the keenest grief I ever felt
Was when my mother beside me knelt,
An' cried an' prayed, till I melted down,
As I wouldn't for half the horses in town.
I kissed her fondly, then an' there,
An' swore henceforth to be honest and square.

I served my sentence—a bitter pill
Some fellows should take who never will;
And then I decided to go "out West,"
Concludin' 'twould suit my health the best;
Where, how I prospered, I never could tell,
But Fortune seemed to like me well,
An' somehow every vein I struck
Was always bubblin' over with luck.
An', better than that, I was steady an' true,
An' put my good resolutions through.
But I wrote to a trusty old neighbor, an' said,
"You tell 'em, old fellow, that I am dead,
An' died a Christian; 'twill please 'em more,
Than if I had lived the same as before."

But when this neighbor he wrote to me,
"Your mother's in the poor-house," says he,
I had a resurrection straightway,
An' started for her that very day.

And when I arrived where I was grown,
I took good care that I shouldn't be known;
But I bought the old cottage, through and through,
Of some one Charley had sold it to;
And held back neither work nor gold,
To fix it up as it was of old.
The same big fire-place wide an' high,
Flung up its cinders toward the sky;
The old clock ticked on the corner-shelf—
I wound it an' set it agoin' myself;
An' if every thing wasn't just the same,
Neither I nor money was to blame;
     Then—*over the hill to the poor-house!*

One blowin', blusterin' winter's day,
With a team an' cutter I started away;
My fiery nags was as black as coal;
(They some'at resembled the horse I stole);
I hitched, an' entered the poor-house door—
A poor old woman was scrubbin' the floor;
She rose to her feet in great surprise,
And looked, quite startled, into my eyes;
I saw the whole of her trouble's trace
In the lines that marred her dear old face;
"Mother!" I shouted, "your sorrows is done!
You're adopted along o' your horse-thief son,
     Come *over the hill from the poor-house!*

She didn't faint; she knelt by my side,
An' thanked the Lord, till I fairly cried.
An' maybe our ride wasn't pleasant an' gay,
An' maybe she wasn't wrapped up that day;
An' maybe our cottage wasn't warm an' bright,
An' maybe it wasn't a pleasant sight,
To see her a-gettin' the evenin's tea,
An' frequently stoppin' and kissin' me;
An' maybe we didn't live happy for years,
In spite of my brothers' and sisters' sneers,

Who often said, as I have heard,
That they wouldn't own a prison-bird;
(Though they're gettin' over that, I guess,
For all of 'em owe me more or less);

But I've learned one thing; an' it cheers a man
In always a-doin' the best he can;
That whether, on the big book, a blot
Gets over a fellow's name or not,
Whenever he does a deed that's white,
It's credited to him fair and right.
An' when you hear the great bugle's notes,
An' the Lord divides his sheep an' goats;
However they may settle my case,
Wherever they may fix my place,
My good old Christian mother, you'll see,
Will be sure to stand right up for me,
　　　　With *over the hill from the poor-house.*

UNCLE SAMMY.

SOME men were born for great things,
    Some were born for small;
    Some—it is not recorded
    Why they were born at all;
But Uncle Sammy was certain he had a legitimate call.

    Some were born with a talent,
    Some with scrip and land;
    Some with a spoon of silver,
    And some with a different brand;
But Uncle Sammy came holding an argument in each hand.

    Arguments sprouted within him,
    And twinked in his little eye;
    He lay and calmly debated
    When average babies cry,
And seemed to be pondering gravely whether to live or to die.

    But prejudiced on that question
    He grew from day to day,
    And finally he concluded
    'Twas better for him to stay;
And so into life's discussion he reasoned and reasoned his way.

    Through childhood, through youth, into manhood
    Argued and argued he;
    And he married a simple maiden,
    Though scarcely in love was she;
But he reasoned the matter so clearly she hardly could help but agree.

And though at first she was blooming,
   And the new firm started strong,
And though Uncle Sammy loved her,
   And tried to help her along,
She faded away in silence, and 'twas evident something was wrong.

Now Uncle Sammy was faithful,
   And various remedies tried;
He gave her the doctor's prescriptions,
   And plenty of logic beside;
But logic and medicine failed him, and so one day she died.

He laid her away in the church-yard,
   So haggard and crushed and wan;
And reared her a costly tombstone
   With all of her virtues on;
And ought to have added, "A victim to arguments pro and con."

For many a year Uncle Sammy
   Fired away at his logical forte:
Discussion was his occupation,
   And altercation his sport;
He argued himself out of churches, he argued himself into court.

But alas for his peace and quiet,
   One day, when he went it blind,
And followed his singular fancy,
   And slighted his logical mind,
And married a ponderous widow that wasn't of the arguing kind!

Her sentiments all were settled,
   Her habits were planted and grown,
Her heart was a starved little creature
   That followed a will of her own;
And she raised a high hand with Sammy, and proceeded to play it alone

Then Sammy he charged down upon her
   With all of his strength and his wit,

"WHO SAT WITH HIM LONG AT HIS TABLE AND EXPLAINED TO HIM WHERE HE STOOD."

And many a dextrous encounter,
And many a fair shoulder-hit;
But vain were his blows and his blowing: he never could budge her a bit.

He laid down his premises round her,
He scraped at her with his saws;
He rained great facts upon her,
And read her the marriage laws;
But the harder he tried to convince her, the harder and harder she was

She brought home all her preachers,
As many as ever she could—
With sentiments terribly settled,
And appetites horribly good—
Who sat with him long at his table, and explained to him where he stood

And Sammy was not long in learning
To follow the swing of her gown,
And came to be faithful in watching
The phase of her smile and her frown;
And she, with the heel of assertion, soon tramped all his arguments down,

And so, with his life-aspirations
Thus suddenly brought to a check—
And so, with the foot of his victor
Unceasingly pressing his neck—
He wrote on his face, "I'm a victim," and drifted—a logical wreck.

And farmers, whom he had argued
To corners tight and fast,
Would wink at each other and chuckle,
And grin at him as he passed,   [last."
As to say, "My ambitious old fellow, your whiffletree's straightened at

Old Uncle Sammy one morning
Lay down on his comfortless bed,
And Death and he had a discussion,
And Death came out ahead;
And the fact that SHE failed to start him was only because he was dead.

The neighbors laid out their old neighbor,
　　With homely but tenderest art;
And some of the oldest ones faltered,
　　And tearfully stood apart;
For the crusty old man had often unguardedly shown them his heart.

But on his face an expression
　　Of quizzical study lay,
As if he were sounding the angel
　　Who traveled with him that day,
And laying the pipes down slyly for an argument on the way.

And one new-fashioned old lady
　　Felt called upon to suggest
That the angel might take Uncle Sammy,
　　And give him a good night's rest,
And then introduce him to Solomon, and tell him to do his best.

TOM WAS GOIN' FOR A POET.

The Farmer Discourses of his Son.

TOM was goin' for a poet, an' said he'd a poet be;
One of these long-haired fellers a feller hates to see;
One of these chaps forever fixin' things cute and clever;
Makin' the world in gen'ral step 'long to tune an' time,
An' cuttin' the earth into slices an' saltin' it down into rhyme.

Poets are good for somethin', so long as they stand at the head;
But poetry's worth whatever it fetches in butter an' bread.
An' many a time I've said it: it don't do a fellow credit,
To starve with a hole in his elbow, an' be considered a fool,
So after he's dead, the young ones 'll speak his pieces in school.

An' Tom, he had an opinion that Shakspeare an' all the rest,
With all their winter clothin', couldn't make *him* a decent vest;
But that didn't ease my labors, or help him among the neighbors,
Who watched him from a distance, an' held his mind in doubt,
An' wondered if Tom wasn't shaky, or knew what he was about.

Tom he went a-sowin', to sow a field of grain;
But half of that 'ere sowin' was altogether in vain.
For he was al'ays a-stoppin', and gems of poetry droppin';
And metaphors, they be pleasant, but much too thin to eat;
And germs of thought be handy, but never grow up to wheat.

Tom he went a-mowin', one broilin' summer's day,
An' spoke quite sweet concernin' the smell of the new-mowed hay.
But all o' his useless chatter didn't go to help the matter,
Or make the grief less searchin' or the pain less hard to feel,
When he made a clip too suddent, an' sliced his brother's heel.

Tom he went a-drivin' the hills an' dales across;
But, scannin' the lines of his poetry, he dropped the lines of his hoss.
The nag ran fleet and fleeter, in quite irregular metre;
An' when we got Tom's leg set, an' had fixed him so he could speak,
He muttered that that adventur' would keep him a-writin' a week.

Tom he went a-ploughin', and couldn't have done it worse;
He sat down on the handles, an' went to spinnin' verse.
He wrote it nice and pretty—an agricultural ditty;
But all o' his pesky measures didn't measure an acre more,
Nor his p'ints didn't turn a furrow that wasn't turned before.

Tom he went a-courtin';—she liked him, I suppose;
But certain parts of courtin' a feller must do in prose.
He rhymed her each day a letter, but that didn't serve to get her;
He waited so long, she married another man from spite,
An' sent him word she'd done it, an' not to forget to write.

Tom at last got married; his wife was smart and stout,
An' she shoved up the window and slung his poetry out.
An' at each new poem's creation she gave it circulation;
An' fast as he would write 'em, she seen to their puttin' forth,
An' sent 'em east an' westward, an' also south an' north.

Till Tom he struck the opinion that poetry didn't pay,
An' turned the guns of his genius, an' fired 'em another way.
He settled himself down steady, an' is quite well off already;
An' all of his life is verses, with his wife the first an' best,
An' ten or a dozen childr'n to constitute the rest.

GOIN' HOME TO-DAY.

MY business on the jury's done—the quibblin' all is through—
I've watched the lawyers right and left, and give my verdict true;
I stuck so long unto my chair, I thought I would grow in;
And if I do not know myself, they'll get me there ag'in;
But now the court's adjourned for good, and I have got my pay;
I'm loose at last, and thank the Lord, I'm going home to-day.

I've somehow felt uneasy like, since first day I come down;
It is an awkward game to play the gentleman in town;
And this 'ere Sunday suit of mine on Sunday rightly sets;
But when I wear the stuff a week, it somehow galls and frets.
I'd rather wear my homespun rig of pepper-salt and gray—
I'll have it on in half a jiff, when I get home to-day.

I have no doubt my wife looked out, as well as any one—
As well as any woman could—to see that things was done:
For though Melinda, when I'm there, won't set her foot outdoors
She's very careful, when I'm gone, to tend to all the chores.
But nothing prospers half so well when I go off to stay,
And I will put things into shape, when I get home to-day.

The mornin' that I come away, we had a little bout;
I coolly took my hat and left, before the show was out.
For what I said was naught whereat she ought to take offense;
And she was always quick at words and ready to commence.
But then she's first one to give up when she has had her say;
And she will meet me with a kiss, when I go home to-day.

My little boy—I'll give 'em leave to match him, if they can;
It's fun to see him strut about, and try to be a man!

The gamest, cheeriest little chap, you'd ever want to see!
And then they laugh, because I think the child resembles me.
The little rogue! he goes for me, like robbers for their prey;
He'll turn my pockets inside out, when I get home to-day.

My little girl—I can't contrive how it should happen thus—
That God could pick that sweet bouquet, and fling it down to us!
My wife, she says that han'some face will some day make a stir;
And then I laugh, because she thinks the child resembles her.
She'll meet me half-way down the hill, and kiss me, any way;
And light my heart up with her smiles, when I go home to-day!

If there's a heaven upon the earth, a fellow knows it when
He's been away from home a week, and then gets back again.
If there's a heaven above the earth, there often, I'll be bound,
Some homesick fellow meets his folks, and hugs 'em all around.
But let my creed be right or wrong, or be it as it may,
My heaven is just ahead of me—I'm going home to-day.

[*As Told in* 1880.]

OUT O' THE FIRE.

YEAR of '71, children, middle of the fall,
On one fearful night, children, we well-nigh lost our all.
True, it wa'n't no great sum we had to lose that night,
But when a little's all you've got, it comes to a blessed sight.

I was a mighty worker, in them 'ere difficult days,
For work is a good investment, and almost always pays;
But when ten years' hard labor went smokin' into the air,
I doubted all o' the maxims, an' felt that it wasn't fair.

Up from the East we had traveled, with all of our household wares,
Where we had long been workin' a piece of land on shares;
But how a fellow's to prosper without the rise of the land,
For just two-thirds of nothin', I never could understand.

Up from the East we had traveled, me and my folks alone,
And quick we went to workin' a piece of land of our own;
Small was our backwoods quarters, and things looked mighty cheap;
But every thing we put in there, we put in there to keep.

So, with workin' and savin', we managed to get along;
Managed to make a livin', and feel consid'able strong;
And things went smooth and happy, an' fair as the average run,
Till every thing went back on me, in the fall of '71.

First thing bothered and worried me, was 'long o' my daughter Kate;
Rather a han'some cre'tur', and folks all liked her gait.
Not so nice as them sham ones in yeller-covered books;
But still there wa'n't much discount on Katherine's ways an' looks.

And Katherine's smile was pleasant, and Katherine's temper good,
And how she come to like Tom Smith, I never understood;
For she was a mornin'-glory, as fair as you ever see,
And Tom was a shag-bark hickory, as green as green could be.

"Like takes to like," is a proverb that's nothin' more than trash;
And many a time I've seen it all pulverized to smash.
For folks in no way sim'lar, I've noticed ag'in and ag'in,
Will often take to each other, and stick together like sin.

Next thing bothered and worried me, was 'long of a terrible drouth;
And me an' all o' my neighbors was some'at down in the mouth.
And week after week the rain held off, and things all pined an' dried,
And we drove the cattle miles to drink, and many of 'em died.

And day after day went by us, so han'some and so bright,
And never a drop of water came near us, day or night;
And what with the neighbors' grumblin', and what with my daily loss,
I must own that somehow or other I was gettin' mighty cross.

And on one Sunday evenin' I was comin' down the lane
From meetin', where our preacher had stuck and hung for rain,
And various slants on heaven kept workin' in my mind,
And the smoke from Sanders' fallow was makin' me almost blind;

I opened the door kind o' sudden, an' there my Katherine sat,
As cozy as any kitten along with a friendly cat;
An' Tom was dreadful near her—his arm on the back of her chair—
And lookin' as happy and cheerful as if there was rain to spare.

"Get out of this house in a minute!" I cried, with all my might:
"Get out, while I'm a-talkin'!"—Tom's eyes showed a bit of fight;
But he rose up, stiff and surly, and made me a civil bow,
And mogged along to the door-way, with never a word of row.

And I snapped up my wife quite surly when she asked me what I'd said,
And I scolded Kate for cryin', and sent her up stairs to bed;
And then I laid down, for the purpose of gettin' a little sleep,
An' the wind outside was a-howlin', and puttin' it in to keep.

'Twas half-past three next mornin', or maybe 'twas nearer four—
The neighbors they came a-yellin' and poundin' at my door;
"Get up! get up!" they shouted: "get up! there's danger near!
The woods are all a-burnin'! the wind is blowin' it here!"

If ever it happens, children, that you get catched, some time,
With fire a-blowin' toward you, as fast as fire can climb,
You'll get up and get in a hurry, as fast as you can budge;
It's a lively season of the year, or else I ain't no judge!

Out o' the dear old cabin we tumbled fast as we could—
Smashed two-thirds of our dishes, and saved some four-foot wood;
With smoke a-settlin' round us and gettin' into our eyes,
And fire a-roarin' an' roarin' an' drowndin' all of our cries.

And just as the roof was smokin', and we hadn't long to wait,
I says to my wife, "Now get out, and hustle, you and Kate!"
And just as the roof was fallin', my wife she come to me,
With a face as white as a corpse's face, and "Where *is* Kate?" says she.

And the neighbors come runnin' to me, with faces black as the ground,
And shouted, "Where is Katherine? She's nowhere to be found!"

*   *   *   *   *   *   *   *   *

An' this is all I remember, till I found myself next day,
A-lyin' in Sanders' cabin, a mile an' a half away.

If ever you wake up, children, with somethin' into your head,
Concernin' a han'some daughter, that's lyin' still an' dead,
All scorched into coal-black cinders—*perhaps* you may not weep,
But I rather think it'll happen you'll wish you'd a-kept asleep.

And all I could say, was "Kath'rine, oh Kath'rine, come to me!"
And all I could think, was "Kath'rine!" and all that I could see,
Was Sanders a-standin' near to me, his finger into his eye,
And my wife a-bendin' over me, and tellin' me not to cry;

When, lo! Tom Smith he entered—his face lit up with grins—
And Kate a-hangin' on his arm, as neat as a row of pins!
And Tom looked glad, but sheepish; and said, "Excuse me, Squire,
But I 'loped with Kate, and married her an hour before the fire."

Well, children, I was shattered; 'twas more than I could bear—
And I up and went for Kate an' Tom, and hugged 'em then and there
And since that time, the times have changed, an' now they ain't so bad
And—Katherine, she's your mother now, and—Thomas Smith's your dad

OTHER POEMS.

OTHER POEMS.

THE NEW CHURCH ORGAN.

THEY'VE got a brand-new organ, Sue,
  For all their fuss and search;
They've done just as they said they'd do,
  And fetched it into church.
They're bound the critter shall be seen,
  And on the preacher's right
They've hoisted up their new machine,
  In every body's sight.
They've got a chorister and choir,
  Ag'in' *my* voice and vote;
For it was never *my* desire,
  To praise the Lord by note!

I've been a sister good an' true
  For five-an'-thirty year;
I've done what seemed my part to do,
  An' prayed my duty clear;
I've sung the hymns both slow and quick,
  Just as the preacher read,
And twice, when Deacon Tubbs was sick,
  I took the fork an' led!
And now, their bold, new-fangled ways
  Is comin' all about;
And I, right in my latter days,
  Am fairly crowded out!

To-day the preacher, good old dear,
 With tears all in his eyes,
Read, "I can read my title clear
 To mansions in the skies."
I al'ays liked that blessed hymn—
 I s'pose I al'ays will;
It somehow gratifies *my* whim,
 In good old Ortonville;
But when that choir got up to sing,
 I couldn't catch a word;
They sung the most dog-gondest thing
 A body ever heard!

Some worldly chaps was standin' near;
 An' when I see them grin,
I bid farewell to every fear,
 And boldly waded in.
I thought I'd chase their tune along,
 An' tried with all my might;
But though my voice is good an' strong,
 I couldn't steer it right;
When they was high, then I was low,
 An' also contrawise;
An' I too fast, or they too slow,
 To "mansions in the skies."

An' after every verse, you know,
 They play a little tune;
I didn't understand, an' so
 I started in too soon.
I pitched it pretty middlin' high,
 I fetched a lusty tone,
But oh, alas! I found that I
 Was singin' there alone!
They laughed a little, I am told;
 But I had done my best;
And not a wave of trouble rolled
 Across my peaceful breast.

And Sister Brown—I could but look—
  She sits right front of me;
She never was no singin'-book,
  An' never went to be;
But then she al'ays tried to do
  The best she could, she said;
She understood the time right through,
  An' kep' it with her head;
But when she tried this mornin', oh.
  I had to laugh, or cough!
It kep' her head a-bobbin' so,
  It e'en a'most came off!

An' Deacon Tubbs—he all broke down,
  As one might well suppose;
He took one look at Sister Brown,
  And meekly scratched his nose.
He looked his hymn-book through and through,
  And laid it on the seat,
And then a pensive sigh he drew,
  And looked completely beat.
An' when they took another bout,
  He didn't even rise;
But drawed his red bandanner out,
  An' wiped his weepin' eyes.

I've been a sister, good an' true,
  For five-an'-thirty year;
I've done what seemed my part to do,
  An' prayed my duty clear;
But Death will stop my voice, I know,
  For he is on my track;
And some day I to church will go,
  And never more come back;
And when the folks gets up to sing—
  Whene'er that time shall be—
I do not want no *patent* thing
  A-squealin' over me!

THE EDITOR'S GUESTS.

THE Editor sat in his sanctum, his countenance furrowed with care,
His mind at the bottom of business, his feet at the top of a chair,
His chair-arm an elbow supporting, his right hand upholding his head,
His eyes on his dusty old table, with different documents spread:
There were thirty 'ong pages from Howler, with underlined capitals topped,
And a short disquisition from Growler, requesting his newspaper stopped;
There were lyrics from Gusher, the poet, concerning sweet flow'rets and
    zephyrs,
And a stray gem from Plodder, the farmer, describing a couple of heifers;
There were billets from beautiful maidens, and bills from a grocer or two,
And his best leader hitched to a letter, which inquired if he wrote it, or
    who?
There were raptures of praises from writers of the weakly mellifluous
    school,
And one of his rival's last papers, informing him he was a fool;
There were several long resolutions, with names telling whom they were
    by,
Canonizing some harmless old brother who had done nothing worse than
    to die;
There were traps on that table to catch him, and serpents to sting and to
    smite him;
There were gift enterprises to sell him, and bitters attempting to bite him;
There were long staring "ads" from the city, and money with never a one,
Which added, "Please give this insertion, and send in your bill when
    you're *done;*"
There were letters from organizations — their meetings, their wants, and
    their laws—
Which said, "Can you print this announcement for the good of our glori-
    ous cause?"
There were tickets inviting his presence to festivals, parties, and shows,
Wrapped in notes with "Please give us a notice" demurely slipped in at
    the close;

In short, as his eye took the table, and ran o'er its ink-spattered trash,
There was nothing it did not encounter, excepting perhaps it was cash.

The Editor dreamily pondered on several ponderous things.
On different lines of action, and the pulling of different strings;
Upon some equivocal doings, and some unequivocal duns;
On how few of his numerous patrons were quietly prompt-paying ones;
On friends who subscribed "just to help him," and wordy encouragement
    lent,
And had given him plenty of counsel, but never had paid him a cent;
On vinegar, kind-hearted people were feeding him every hour,
Who saw not the work they were doing, but wondered that "printers are
    sour:"
On several intelligent townsmen, whose kindness was so without stint
That they kept an eye out on his business, and told him just what he
    should print;
On men who had rendered him favors, and never pushed forward their
    claims,
So long as the paper was crowded with "locals" containing their names;
On various other small matters, sufficient his temper to roil,
And finely contrived to be making the blood of an editor boil;
And so one may see that his feelings could hardly be said to be smooth,
And he needed some pleasant occurrence his ruffled emotions to soothe:
He had it; for lo! on the threshold, a slow and reliable tread,
And a farmer invaded the sanctum, and these are the words that he said:

"Good-mornin', sir, Mr. Printer; how is your body to-day?
I'm glad you're to home; for you fellers is al'ays a runnin' away.
Your paper last week wa'n't so spicy nor sharp as the one week before:
But I s'pose when the campaign is opened, you'll be whoopin' it up to 'em
    more.
That feller that's printin' *The Smasher* is goin' for you perty smart;
And our folks said this mornin' at breakfast, they thought he was gettin
    the start.
But I hushed 'em right up in a minute, and said a good word for you;
I told 'em I b'lieved you was tryin' to do just as well as you knew;
And I told 'em that some one was sayin', and whoever 'twas it is so,
That you can't expect much of no one man, nor blame him for what he
    don't know.

But, layin' aside *pleasure* for business, I've brought you my little boy Jim;
And I thought I would see if you couldn't make an editor outen of him.

"My family stock is increasin', while other folks' seems to run short.
I've got a right smart of a family—it's one of the old-fashioned sort:
There's Ichabod, Isaac, and Israel, a-workin' away on the farm—
They do 'bout as much as one good boy, and make things go off like a
　　　charm.
There's Moses and Aaron are sly ones, and slip like a couple of eels;
But they're tol'able steady in one thing—they al'ays git round to their
　　　meals.
There's Peter is busy inventin' (though *what* he invents I can't see),
And Joseph is studyin' medicine—and both of 'em boardin' with me.
There's Abram and Albert is married, each workin' my farm for himself,
And Sam smashed his nose at a shootin', and so he is laid on the shelf.
The rest of the boys are all growin', 'cept this little runt, which is Jim,
And I thought that perhaps I'd be makin' an editor outen o' him.

"He ain't no great shakes for to labor, though I've labored with him a
　　　good deal,
And give him some strappin' good arguments I know he couldn't help but
　　　to feel;
But he's built out of second-growth timber, and nothin' about him is big
Exceptin' his appetite only, and there he's as good as a pig.
I keep him a-carryin' luncheons, and fillin' and bringin' the jugs,
And take him among the pertatoes, and set him to pickin' the bugs;
And then there is things to be doin' a-helpin' the women indoors;
There's churnin' and washin' of dishes, and other descriptions of chores;
But he don't take to nothin' but victuals, and he'll never be much, I'm
　　　afraid,
So I thought it would be a good notion to larn him the editor's trade.
His body's too small for a farmer, his judgment is rather too slim,
But I thought we perhaps could be makin' an editor outen o' him!

"It ain't much to get up a paper—it wouldn't take him long for to learn;
He could feed the machine, I'm thinkin', with a good strappin' fellow to turn.
And things that was once hard in doin', is easy enough now to do;
Just keep your eye on your machinery, and crack your arrangements right
　　　through.

I used for to wonder at readin', and where it was got up, and how;
But 'tis most of it made by machinery—I can see it all plain enough now.
And poetry, too, is constructed by machines of different designs,
Each one with a gauge and a chopper to see to the length of the lines;
And I hear a New York clairvoyant is runnin' one sleeker than grease,
And *a-rentin'* her heaven-born productions at a couple of dollars apiece;
An' since the whole trade has growed easy, 'twould be easy enough, I've
    a whim,
If you was agreed, to be makin' an editor outen of Jim!"

The Editor sat in his sanctum and looked the old man in the eye,
Then glanced at the grinning young hopeful, and mournfully made his
    reply:
"Is your son a small unbound edition of Moses and Solomon both?
Can he compass his spirit with meekness, and strangle a natural oath?
Can he leave all his wrongs to the future, and carry his heart in his cheek?
Can he do an hour's work in a minute, and live on a sixpence a week?
Can he courteously talk to an equal, and browbeat an impudent dunce?
Can he keep things in apple-pie order, and do half a dozen at once?
Can he press all the springs of knowledge, with quick and reliable touch,
And be sure that he knows how much *to* know, and knows how to not
    know too much?
Does he know how to spur up his virtue, and put a check-rein on his
    pride?
Can he carry a gentleman's manners within a rhinoceros' hide?
Can he know all, and do all, and be all, with cheerfulness, courage, and
    vim?
If so, we perhaps can be makin an editor 'outen of him.' "

The farmer stood curiously listening, while wonder his visage o'erspread;
And he said, "Jim, I guess we'll be goin'; he's probably out of his head."

But lo! on the rickety stair-case, another reliable tread,
And entered another old farmer, and these are the words that *he* said:

"Good-morning, sir, Mr. Editor, how is the folks to-day?
I owe you for next year's paper; I thought I'd come in and pay.
And Jones is agoin' to take it, and this is his money here;
I shut down on lendin' it to him, and coaxed him to try it a year.

And here is a few little items that happened last week in our town:
I thought they'd look good for the paper, and so I just jotted 'em down.
And here is a basket of cherries my wife picked expressly for you;
And a small bunch of flowers from Jennie—she thought she must send
    somethin' too.
You're doin' the politics bully, as all of our family agree;
Just keep your old goose-quill a-floppin', and give 'em a good one for me.
And now you are chuck full of business, and I won't be takin' your time;
I've things of my own I must 'tend to — good-day, sir, I b'lieve I will
    climb."

The Editor sat in his sanctum and brought down his fist with a thump:
"God bless that old farmer," he muttered, "he's a regular Editor's trump."

And 'tis thus with our noble profession, and thus it will ever be, still;
There are some who appreciate its labors, and some who perhaps never
    will.
But in the great time that is coming, when loudly the trumpet shall sound,
And they who have labored and rested shall come from the quivering
    ground;
When they who have striven and suffered to teach and ennoble the race,
Shall march at the front of the column, each one in his God-given place,
As they pass through the gates of The City with proud and victorious
    tread,
The editor, printer, and "devil," will travel not far from the head.

THE HOUSE WHERE WE WERE WED.

I'VE been to the old farm-house, good-wife,
  Where you and I were wed;
Where the love was born to our two hearts
  That now lies cold and dead.
Where a long-kept secret to you I told,
  In the yellow beams of the moon,
And we forged our vows out of love's own gold,
  To be broken so soon, so soon!

I passed through all the old rooms, good-wife;
  I wandered on and on;
I followed the steps of a flitting ghost,
  The ghost of a love that is gone.
And he led me out to the arbor, wife,
  Where with myrtles I twined your hair;
And he seated me down on the old stone step,
  And left me musing there.

The sun went down as it used to do,
  And sunk in the sea of night;
The two bright stars that we called ours
  Came slowly unto my sight;
But the one that was mine went under a cloud—
  Went under a cloud, alone;
And a tear that I wouldn't have shed for the world,
  Fell down on the old gray stone.

But there be words can ne'er be unsaid,
  And deeds can ne'er be undone,

Except perhaps in another world,
   Where life's once more begun.
And maybe some time in the time to come.
   When a few more years are sped,
We'll love again as we used to love,
   In the house where we were wed.

OUR ARMY OF THE DEAD.

By the edge of the Atlantic, where the waves of Freedom roar,
And the breezes of the ocean chant a requiem to the shore,
On the Nation's eastern hill-tops, where its corner-stone is laid,
On the mountains of New England, where our fathers toiled and prayed,
Mid old Key-stone's rugged riches, which the miner's hand await,
Mid the never-ceasing commerce of the busy Empire State,
With the country's love and honor on each brave, devoted head,
Is a band of noble heroes—is our Army of the Dead.

On the lake-encircled homestead of the thriving Wolverine,
On the beauteous Western prairies, with their carpeting of green,
By the sweeping Mississippi, long our country's pride and boast,
On the rugged Rocky Mountains, and the weird Pacific coast,
In the listless, sunny Southland, with its blossoms and its vines,
On the bracing Northern hill-tops, and amid their murmuring pines,
Over all our happy country—over all our Nation spread,
Is a band of noble heroes—is our Army of the Dead.

Not with musket, and with sabre, and with glad heart beating fast;
Not with cannon that had thundered till the bloody war was past;
Not with voices that are shouting with the vim of victory's note;
Not with armor gayly glistening, and with flags that proudly float;
Not with air of martial vigor, nor with steady, soldier tramp,
Come they grandly marching to us—for the boys are all in camp.
With forgetfulness upon it—each within his earthy bed,
Waiting for his marching orders—is our Army of the Dead.

Fast asleep the boys are lying, in their low and narrow tents,
And no battle-cry can wake them, and no orders call them hence;
And the yearnings of the mother, and the anguish of the wife,
Can not with their magic presence call the soldier back to life;

And the brother's manly sorrow, and the father's mournful pride,
Can not give back to his country him who for his country died.
They who for the trembling Nation in its hour of trial bled,
Lie, in these its years of triumph, with our Army of the Dead.

When the years of Earth are over, and the cares of Earth are done,
When the reign of Time is ended, and Eternity begun,
When the thunders of Omniscience on our wakened senses roll,
And the sky above shall wither, and be gathered like a scroll;
When, among the lofty mountains, and across the mighty sea,
The sublime celestial bugler shall ring out the reveille,
Then shall march with brightest laurels, and with proud, victorious tread,
To their station up in heaven, our Grand Army of the Dead!

APPLE-BLOSSOMS.

UNDERNEATH an apple-tree
  Sat a maiden and her lover;
And the thoughts within her he
  Yearned, in silence, to discover.
Round them danced the sunbeams bright,
  Green the grass-lawn stretched before them;
While the apple-blossoms white
  Hung in rich profusion o'er them.

Naught within her eyes he read
  That would tell her mind unto him;
Though their light, he after said,
  Quivered swiftly through and through him;
Till at last his heart burst free
  From the prayer with which 'twas laden,
And he said, "When wilt thou be
  Mine for evermore, fair maiden?"

"When," said she, "the breeze of May
  With white flakes our heads shall cover,
I will be thy brideling gay—
  Thou shalt be my husband-lover."
"How," said he, in sorrow bowed,
  "Can I hope such hopeful weather?
Breeze of May and Winter's cloud
  Do not often fly together."

Quickly as the words he said,
  From the west a wind came sighing,

And on each uncovered head
  Sent the apple-blossoms flying;
"'Flakes of white!' thou'rt mine," said he,
  "Sooner than thy wish or knowing!"
"Nay, I heard the breeze," quoth she,
  "When in yonder forest blowing."

APPLES GROWING.

UNDERNEATH an apple-tree
  Sat a dame of comely seeming,
With her work upon her knee,
  And her great eyes idly dreaming.
O'er the harvest-acres bright,
  Came her husband's din of reaping;
Near to her, an infant wight
  Through the tangled grass was creeping.

On the branches long and high,
  And the great green apples growing,
Rested she her wandering eye,
  With a retrospective knowing.
"This," she said, "the shelter is,
  Where, when gay and raven-headed,
I consented to be his,
  And our willing hearts were wedded.

"Laughing words and peals of mirth,
  Long are changed to grave endeavor;
Sorrow's winds have swept to earth
  Many a blossomed hope forever.
Thunder-heads have hovered o'er—
  Storms my path have chilled and shaded;
Of the bloom my gay youth bore,
  Some has fruited—more has faded."

Quickly, and amid her sighs,
  Through the grass her baby wrestled,

Smiled on her its father's eyes,
  And unto her bosom nestled.
And with sudden, joyous glee,
  Half the wife's and half the mother's,
"Still the best is left," said she:
  "I have learned to live for others."

ONE AND TWO.

I.

IF you to me be cold,
  Or I be false to you,
The world will go on, I think,
  Just as it used to do;
The clouds will flirt with the moon,
  The sun will kiss the sea,
The wind to the trees will whisper,
  And laugh at you and me;
But the sun will not shine so bright,
The clouds will not seem so white,
  To one, as they will to two;
So I think you had better be kind,
  And I had best be true,
And let the old love go on,
  Just as it used to do.

II.

If the whole of a page be read,
  If a book be finished through,
Still the world may read on, I think,
  Just as it used to do;
For other lovers will con
  The pages that we have passed,
And the treacherous gold of the binding
  Will glitter unto the last.
But lids have a lonely look,
And one may not read the book—
  It opens only to two;

So I think you had better be kind,
  And I had best be true,
And let the reading go on,
  Just as it used to do.

III.

If we who have sailed together
  Flit out of each other's view,
The world will sail on, I think,
  Just as it used to do;
And we may reckon by stars
  That flash from different skies,
And another of love's pirates
  May capture my lost prize;
But ships long time together
Can better the tempest weather
  Than any other two;
So I think you had better be kind,
  And I had best be true,
That we together may sail,
  Just as we used to do.

THE FADING FLOWER.

THERE is a chillness in the air—
  A coldness in the smile of day;
And e'en the sunbeam's crimson glare
  Seems shaded with a tinge of gray.

Weary of journeys to and fro,
  The sun low creeps adown the sky;
And on the shivering earth below,
  The long, cold shadows grimly lie.

But there will fall a deeper shade,
  More chilling than the Autumn's breath:
There is a flower that yet must fade,
  And yield its sweetness up to death.

She sits upon the window-seat,
  Musing in mournful silence there,
While on her brow the sunbeams meet,
  And dally with her golden hair.

She gazes on the sea of light
  That overflows the western skies,
Till her great soul seems plumed for flight
  From out the window of her eyes.

Hopes unfulfilled have vexed her breast,
  Sad smiles have checked the rising sigh;
Until her weary heart confessed,
  Reluctantly, that she must die.
7

And she has thought of all the ties—
  The golden ties—that bind her here;
Of all that she has learned to prize,
  Of all that she has counted dear;

The joys of body, heart, and mind,
  The pleasures that she loves so well;
The grasp of friendship, warm and kind,
  And love's delicious, hallowed spell.

And she has wept, that she must lie
  Beneath the snow-wreaths, drifted deep,
With no fond mother standing nigh,
  To watch her in her silent sleep.

And she has prayed, if it might be
  Within the reach of human skill,
And not averse to Heaven, that she
  Might live a little longer still.

But earthly hope is gone; and now
  Comes in its place a brighter beam,
Leaving upon her snowy brow
  The impress of a heavenly dream:

That she, when her frail body yields,
  And fades away to mortal eyes,
Shall burst through Heaven's eternal fields,
  And bloom again—in Paradise.

AUTUMN DAYS.

YELLOW, mellow, ripened days,
  Sheltered in a golden coating;
O'er the dreamy, listless haze,
  White and dainty cloudlets floating;
Winking at the blushing trees,
  And the sombre, furrowed fallow;
Smiling at the airy ease
  Of the southward-flying swallow.
Sweet and smiling are thy ways,
Beauteous, golden, Autumn days!

Shivering, quivering, tearful days,
  Fretfully and sadly weeping;
Dreading still, with anxious gaze,
  Icy fetters round thee creeping;
O'er the cheerless, withered plain,
  Woefully and hoarsely calling;
Pelting hail and drenching rain
  On thy scanty vestments falling.
Sad and mournful are thy ways.
Grieving, wailing, Autumn days!

DEATH-DOOMED.

THEY'RE taking me to the gallows, mother—they mean to hang me high;
They're going to gather round me there, and watch me till I die;
All earthly joy has vanished now, and gone each mortal hope,—
They'll draw a cap across my eyes, and round my neck a rope;
The crazy mob will shout and groan—the priest will read a prayer,
The drop will fall beneath my feet and leave me in the air.
They think I murdered Allen Bayne; for so the Judge has said,
And they'll hang me to the gallows, mother—hang me till I'm dead!

The grass that grows in yonder meadow, the lambs that skip and play,
The pebbled brook behind the orchard, that laughs upon its way,
The flowers that bloom in the dear old garden, the birds that sing and fly,
Are clear and pure of human blood, and, mother, so am I!
By father's grave on yonder hill—his name without a stain—
I ne'er had malice in my heart, or murdered Allen Bayne!
But twelve good men have found me guilty, for so the Judge has said,
And they'll hang me to the gallows, mother—hang me till I'm dead!

The air is fresh and bracing, mother; the sun shines bright and high;
It is a pleasant day to live—a gloomy one to die!
It is a bright and glorious day the joys of earth to grasp—
It is a sad and wretched one to strangle, choke, and gasp!
But let them damp my lofty spirit, or cow me if they can!
They send me like a rogue to death—I'll meet it like a man;
For I never murdered Allen Bayne! but so the Judge has said,
And they'll hang me to the gallows, mother—hang me till I'm dead!

Poor little sister 'Bell will weep, and kiss me as I lie;
But kiss her twice and thrice for me, and tell her not to cry;
Tell her to weave a bright, gay garland, and crown me as of yore,
Then plant a lily upon my grave, and think of me no more.

And tell that maiden whose love I sought, that I was faithful yet;
But I must lie in a felon's grave, and she had best forget.
My memory is stained forever; for so the Judge has said,
And they'll hang me to the gallows, mother—hang me till I'm dead!

Lay me not down by my father's side; for once, I mind, he said
No child that stained his spotless name should share his mortal bed.
Old friends would look beyond his grave, to my dishonored one,
And hide the virtues of the sire behind the recreant son.
And I can fancy, if there my corse its fettered limbs should lay,
His frowning skull and crumbling bones would shrink from me away,
But I swear to God I'm innocent, and never blood have shed!
And they'll hang me to the gallows, mother—hang me till I'm dead!

Lay me in my coffin, mother, as you've sometimes seen me rest:
One of my arms beneath my head, the other on my breast.
Place my Bible upon my heart—nay, mother, do not weep—
And kiss me as in happier days you kissed me when asleep.
And for the rest—for form or rite—but little do I reck;
But cover up that cursèd stain—*the black mark on my neck!*
And pray to God for his great mercy on my devoted head;
For they'll hang me to the gallows, mother—hang me till I'm dead!

* * * * * * *

But hark! I hear a mighty murmur among the jostling crowd!
A cry!—a shout!—a roar of voices!—it echoes long and loud!
There dashes a horseman with foaming steed and tightly-gathered rein!
He sits erect!—he waves his hand!—good Heaven! 'tis Allen Bayne!
The lost is found, the dead alive, my safety is achieved!
For he waves his hand again, and shouts, "The prisoner is reprieved!"
Now, mother, praise the God you love, and raise your drooping head;
For the murderous gallows, black and grim, is cheated of its dead!

UP THE LINE.

THROUGH blinding storm and clouds of night,
We swiftly pushed our restless flight;
With thundering hoof and warning neigh,
We urged our steed upon his way
    Up the line.

Afar the lofty head-light gleamed;
Afar the whistle shrieked and screamed;
And glistening bright, and rising high,
Our flakes of fire bestrewed the sky,
    Up the line.

Adown the long, complaining track,
Our wheels a message hurried back;
And quivering through the rails ahead,
Went news of our resistless tread,
    Up the line.

The trees gave back our din and shout,
And flung their shadow arms about;
And shivering in their coats of gray,
They heard us roaring far away,
    Up the line.

The wailing storm came on apace,
And dashed its tears into our face;
But steadily still we pierced it through,
And cut the sweeping wind in two,
    Up the line.

A rattling rush across the ridge,
A thunder-peal beneath the bridge;

And valley and hill and sober plain
Re-echoed our triumphant strain,
     Up the line.

And when the Eastern streaks of gray
Bespoke the dawn of coming day,
We halted our steed, his journey o'er,
And urged his giant form no more,
     Up the line.

HOW WE KEPT THE DAY.

I.

THE great procession came up the street,
With clatter of hoofs and tramp of feet;
There was General Jones to guide the van,
And Corporal Jinks, his right-hand man;
And each was riding his high horse,
And each had epaulettes, of course;
And each had a sash of the bloodiest red,
And each had a shako on his head;
And each had a sword by his left side,
And each had his mustache newly dyed;
   And that was the way
   We kept the day,
The great, the grand, the glorious day,
That gave us—
   Hurray! Hurray! Hurray!
(With a battle or two, the histories say,)
   Our National Independence!

II.

The great procession came up the street,
With loud da capo, and brazen repeat;
There was Hans, the leader, a Teuton born,
A sharp who worried the E flat horn;
And Baritone Jake, and Alto Mike,
Who never played any thing twice alike;
And Tenor Tom, of conservative mind,
Who always came out a note behind;
And Dick, whose tuba was seldom dumb,
And Bob, who punished the big bass drum.

And when they stopped a minute to rest,
The martial band discoursed its best;
The ponderous drum and the pointed fife
Proceeded to roll and shriek for life;
And Bonaparte Crossed the Rhine, anon,
And The Girl I Left Behind Me came on
    And that was the way
    The bands did play
On the loud, high-toned, harmonious day,
That gave us—
    Hurray! Hurray! Hurray!
(With some music of bullets, our sires would say,)
    Our glorious Independence!

III.

The great procession came up the street,
With a wagon of virgins, sour and sweet;
Each bearing the bloom of recent date,
Each misrepresenting a single State.
There was California, pious and prim,
And Louisiana, humming a hymn;
The Texas lass was the smallest one—
Rhode Island weighed the tenth of a ton;
The Empire State was pure as a pearl,
And Massachusetts a modest girl;
Vermont was red as the blush of a rose—
And the goddess sported a turn-up nose;
And looked, free sylph, where she painfully sat,
The worlds she would give to be out of that.
    And in this way
    The maidens gay
Flashed up the street on the beautiful day,
That gave us—
    Hurray! Hurray! Hurray!
(With some sacrifices, our mothers would say,)
    Our glorious Independence!

IV.

The great procession came up the street,
With firemen uniformed flashily neat;
There was Tubbs, the foreman, with voice like five,
The happiest, proudest man alive;
With a trumpet half as long as a gun,
Which he used for the glory of "Number 1;"
There was Nubbs, who had climbed a ladder high,
And saved a dog that was left to die;
There was Cubbs, who had dressed in black and blue
The eye of the foreman of Number 2.
And each marched on with steady stride,
And each had a look of fiery pride;
And each glanced slyly round, with a whim
That all of the girls were looking at him;
   And that was the way,
   With grand display,
They marched through the blaze of the glowing day,
That gave us—
   Hurray! Hurray! Hurray!
(With some hot fighting, our fathers would say,)
   Our glorious Independence!

V.

The eager orator took the stand,
In the cause of our great and happy land;
He aired his own political views,
He told us all of the latest news:
How the Boston folks one night took tea—
Their grounds for steeping it in the sea;
What a heap of Britons our fathers did kill,
At the little skirmish of Bunker Hill;
He put us all in anxious doubt
As to how that matter was coming out;
And when at last he had fought us through
To the bloodless year of '82,

'Twas the fervent hope of every one
That he, as well as the war, was done.
But he continued to painfully soar
For something less than a century more;
Until at last he had fairly begun
The wars of eighteen-sixty-one;
And never rested till 'neath the tree
That shadowed the glory of Robert Lee.
And then he inquired, with martial frown,
"Americans, must we go down?"
And as an answer from Heaven were sent,
The stand gave way, and down he went.
A singer or two beneath him did drop—
A big fat alderman fell atop;
      And that was the way
      Our orator lay,
Till we fished him out, on the eloquent day,
That gave us—
      Hurray! Hurray! Hurray!
(With a clash of arms, Pat. Henry would say,)
      Our wordy Independence!

VI.

The marshal his hungry compatriots led,
Where Freedom's viands were thickly spread,
With all that man or woman could eat,
From crisp to sticky—from sour to sweet.
There were chickens that scarce had learned to crow,
And veteran roosters of long ago;
There was one old turkey, huge and fierce,
That was hatched in the days of President Pierce;
Of which, at last, with an ominous groan,
The parson essayed to swallow a bone;
And it took three sinners, plucky and stout,
To grapple the evil and bring it out.
And still the dinner went merrily on,
And James and Lucy and Hannah and John

Kept winking their eyes and smacking their lips,
And passing the eatables into eclipse.
            And that was the way
            The grand array
Of victuals vanished on that day,
That gave us—
            Hurray! Hurray! Hurray!
(With some starvation, the records say,)
            Our well-fed Independence!

VII.

The people went home through the sultry night,
In a murky mood and a pitiful plight;
Not more had the rockets' sticks gone down,
Than the spirits of them who had "been to town;"
Not more did the fire-balloon collapse,
Than the pride of them who had known mishaps.
There were feathers ruffled, and tempers roiled,
And several brand-new dresses spoiled;
There were hearts that ached from envy's thorns,
And feet that twinged with trampled corns;
There were joys proved empty, through and through,
And several purses empty, too;
And some reeled homeward, muddled and late,
Who hadn't taken their glory straight;
And some were fated to lodge, that night,
In the city lock-up, snug and tight:
            And that was the way
            The deuce was to pay,
As it always is, at the close of the day,
That gave us—
            Hurray! Hurray! Hurray!
(With some restrictions, the fault-finders say,)
That which, please God, we will keep for aye—
            Our National Independence!

Printed in the United States
148853LV00001B/118/A

9 781557 095794